SUPER SPORTS

All-Terrain Bikes

DAVID JEFFERIS

RAINTREE
STECK-VAUGHN
PUBLISHERS

A Harcourt Company

Austin   New York
www.raintreesteckvaughn.com

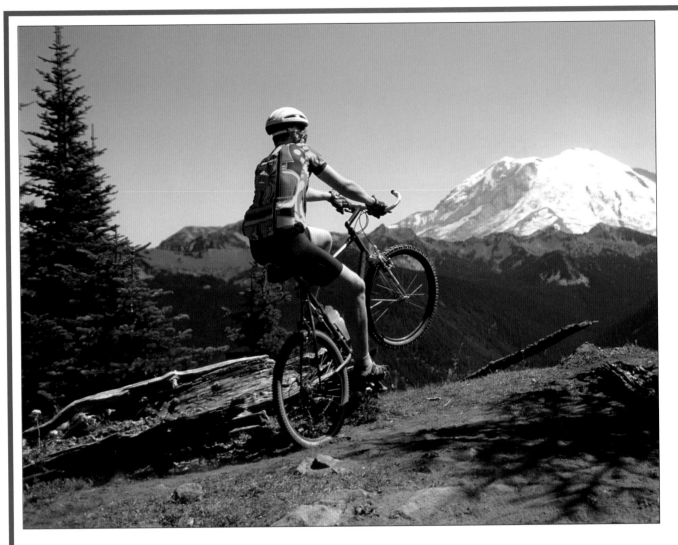

Published by Raintree Steck-Vaughn Publishers, an imprint of Steck-Vaughn Company

Library of Congress Cataloging-in-Publication Data

Jefferis, David.
    All-terrain biking / David Jefferis.
        p. cm. -- (Super sports)
    Includes bibliographical references and index.
    ISBN 0-7398-4345-1
    1. All terrain bicycles--Juvenile literature. 2. All terrain cycling--Juvenile literature. [1. All terrain bicycles. 2. All terrain cycling.] I. Title. II. Super sports (Austin, Tex.)

TL437.5.A43 J44 2001
796.6'3--dc21   2001019202

Acknowledgments
We wish to thank the following individuals and organizations for their help and assistance and for supplying material in their collections:
Action-Plus Photographic, Actionsnaps, Alpha Archive, Steve Bardens, Stewart Clarke, John Cleare, Matt Dickinson, DPPI, Darren England, Malcolm Fearon, Mike Hewitt, Mountain Camera Picture Library, Network Photographers, Gary Pearl, Mike Powell, Adam Pretty, Ben Radford, Jamie Squire, Michael Steele, Dave Stewart, Stock Shot, Joel Tribhout, F. Wagner, Nick Yates

Diagrams by Gavin Page

Printed in China and bound
in the United States.

1 2 3 4 5 6 7 05 04 03 02 01

▲ An all-terrain bike rider makes his bike do a "wheelie" by lifting it off its front wheel.

Contents

 Look out for the Super Sports symbol

Look for the cyclist symbol in boxes like this.
Here you will find extra all-terrain bike facts,
stories, and useful tips for beginners.

World of All-Terrain Bikes

▲ Some events test a rider's control of the bike at slow speeds.

All-terrain bikes are also called mountain bikes. They are sturdily built for riding on dirt trails and in the rural areas.

All-terrain bikes, or ATBs, were first made in the 1970s. They were used for racing along dirt trails in the hills near San Francisco.

Since then ATBs have taken over the cycling world. Today eight out of ten new bikes made are ATBs. They are used by commuters, weekend riders, explorers, and for racing.

▲ Many riders don't want to race. They just enjoy a ride in the fresh air.

◀ Downhill races are held all year round. This rider is going down a snowy mountain slope.

▲ Cross-country races are across all sorts of difficult terrain, including streams and rivers.

◀ Mid-air jumps make ATB racing a great sport to watch. Here riders in a downhill event leap past red marker poles.

Looking at ATBs

There are hundreds of different types of all-terrain bikes, but they are all designed to be used on rough, uneven surfaces.

The main part of an ATB is the frame. It is very strong and usually made of a metal, such as steel or aluminum. The frame supports other parts of the bike, such as the handlebars, wheels, and pedals.

When bikes were made mostly for riding on roads, tires and spokes were enough to cope with most bumps. ATBs are built for use on rougher ground, and many now have shock absorbers for the front or for both wheels. These make riding much smoother.

▲ Many ATBs have front shock absorbers. (See arrow.) These have springs inside that absorb the shock of hitting a bump.

▲ 1950s cruiser bike.
▼ 2000s ATB bike.

Bicycles old and new

Today's ATB is very different from a bike made in the 1950s.

The cruiser bike (top left) was built for cycling in the streets. It has fat tires, but the ATB's tires (below left) also have chunky treads, for gripping dirt trails.

The cruiser bike has brakes that would not hold an ATB for a moment on a steep dirt slope. Today's machine has disc brakes, for much better stopping power, especially when a trail is muddy.

6

▲ Handlebar levers control the brakes. It's best to keep two fingers over each lever so you can brake quickly.

chain from pedals to rear wheel

▲ ATBs have tires with deep grooves for riding off the roads. The tires dig into the soft ground to give a good grip.

▶ Most ATBs have 18 or 21 gears. Low gears are for starting off and for cycling up hills. High gears are for moving fast on flat ground.

Ready to Ride

Before a trip, an all-terrain bike needs to be checked over. This includes pumping air into the tires and oiling various parts.

If one of the bike's moving parts fails, you may have to cut your ride short and go home. So a well-prepared ATB rider has a set of tools and checks over the bike before setting off on a long run.

Punctures can happen, so it's important to take a tire repair kit along, including an air pump.

▲ This ATB is ready to go! The tires are pumped up and the moving parts greased and oiled.

▼ A puncture repair kit should always be taken. Some riders use a spray can of foam to fill a hole in emergency.

aerosol can fills
tire with foam

puncture
repair kit

mini-pump fills a tire
with air quickly

▲ On a warm summer day, a wet rider can dry off quickly. In winter, it's best to ride slower, to avoid being soaked in icy water.

 Carrying an ATB

Cycling off the roads means that there are times when a rider has to get off the bike and carry it—perhaps to cross a stream or to climb a section that's too steep to ride.

The best way to carry an ATB is to bend your legs and put your arm under the top tube. Then straighten up with the bike resting on one shoulder.

top tube

On the Trail

All-terrain biking may take riders a long way from home. So it's necessary to pack food and water, and a map to avoid getting lost.

▲ Car roof racks are useful for taking ATBs to and from the trails.

Riding a new trail is exciting, but it's best to do some research first. An up-to-date map is important, and it's worth checking that the planned route is open. Some trails may be closed to ATBs, especially in popular tourist spots.

Even on a short ride, riders should take food and drink. A small medical kit is also useful so cuts and scrapes can be treated quickly.

▼ Take a map, beverage, and food. Add a basic first-aid kit, just in case. A small camera is useful if the route is in a scenic area.

pen to mark route

water

up-to-date map

chocolate or energy bars

wrap food in foil

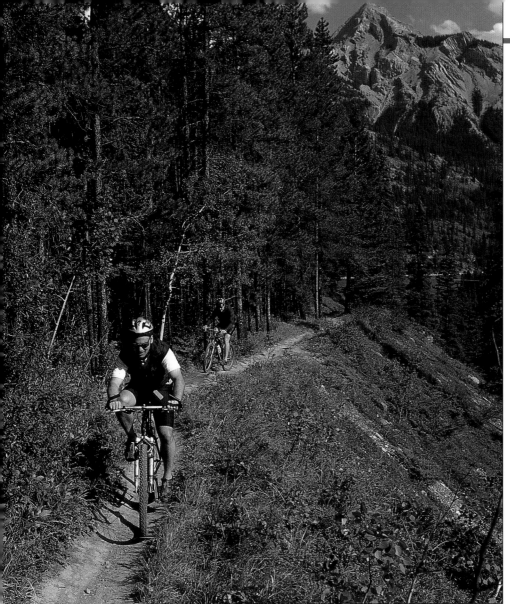

A narrow trail in the Rocky Mountains is an exciting ride. This is just a day trip, so the riders have no camping gear with them.

Even a simple camera can give good results if the view is good.

Photograph time

ATBs are great for getting away from cities and into rural areas. A camera is handy for recording surprise moments, such as the sunset shown here.

Riders should make sure that both front and rear lights are working. A return trip may be on roads in fading light, so lights will be needed for safety.

Safe Riding

Staying safe is important when you're cycling. Keep your eyes on the trail, be careful on steep slopes, and wear a helmet.

▲ Sunglasses keep dust and insects out of the eyes. They also reduce eyestrain.

The simplest way to avoid a fall is to check the trail ahead for dangers. Look out for loose or slippery surfaces on bends and finish braking before making a turn, so that the tires don't lose their grip on the surface.

The best way to tackle a steep downhill section is to shift your body back and use the front brake to control your speed. If it still seems too steep, get off and walk!

◀ Steep sections can be ridden quickly but safely. The back brake does not work well downhill. The front brake helps the rider control the speed.

rider shifts back, to put his weight behind the saddle

▲ If you are carrying an ATB near water, keep it on the side nearest the land.

Fighting the cold

Riding an all-terrain bike in winter is fun, but it can get chilly. A good way to warm cold fingers is by shaking them as if you are trying to shake water off. Stamping cold feet usually warms them up, but don't wear extra socks. Cramped shoes cut off blood circulation, so your feet get colder, not warmer.

Adventure Ride

Day trips and weekend rides are not enough for some bikers. They like to go exploring far from home on their all-terrain bikes.

▲ Riders need to be very careful near steep slopes or cliff tops.

It can be very exciting to go on a long trip to a distant place. The record is held by ATB riders who went from Britain to Australia, a distance of nearly 16,777 miles (27,000 km).

The journey, across Europe and Asia, raised over $21,525 for charity. The riders survived blizzards and earthquakes. There was even a shipwreck when their ATBs were carried on a sailing ship!

▶ An ATB rider cycles across a stony plain, towards the Andes Mountains in Peru, South America.

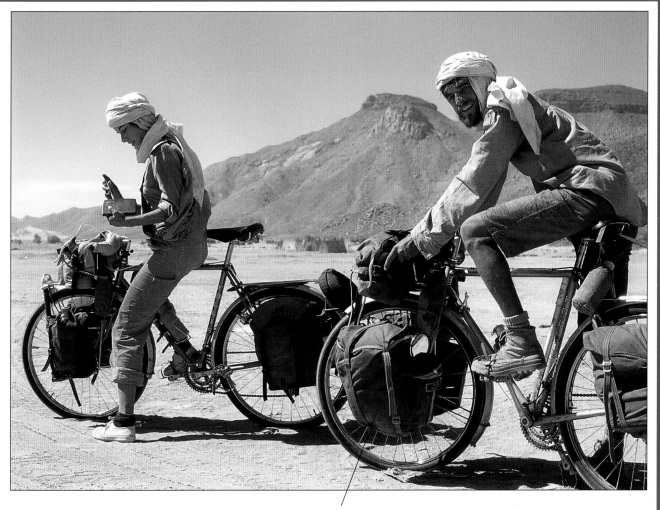

*saddle bags
carry gear*

▲ Riders protect their heads from
the sun in Africa's Sahara Desert.

Covering the miles

Planning for any trip means allowing
enough time to cover the distance. That
includes thinking about the wind and
weather, as well as the terrain.

A cyclist in good shape can cover about
75 miles (120 km) a day on smooth roads.
On dirt tracks, 50-62 miles (80-100 km) is
good. On a muddy trail, it can be half of this.

Downhill Races

Off-road racing is a popular sport. High-speed downhill races are among the most exciting to watch.

Downhill races are over in a few minutes. Racers push their pedals down hard to speed along at 37 miles per hour (60 kmph) or even faster. Courses range from tracks through dark and muddy forests to trails down summer ski slopes. Planners of downhill events often build sharp bends and steep ramps on the trail to add excitement to the race.

◄ This racing ATB has a disc brake, for extra stopping power on a downhill course in France.

▲ Downhill racers crash often, so full-face helmets are worn for good head protection.

◀ Tires slip and slide on loose gravel and stony surfaces, so riders use care on high-speed bends.

 Slipping and sliding

The weather makes a big difference to downhill racing times. One rider in a competition in Switzerland said, "Fog and thunderstorms wrecked my racing times. I took four minutes to go down the hill when we practiced in dry weather. By the time we raced, heavy rain had turned the track into slimy mud. Now I took over six minutes to race down!"

▲ Close-fitting glasses keep dust out of this rider's eyes.

Cross-Country

Cross-country races take riders across routes that are so difficult that sometimes the bikes have to be carried.

Cross-country racing only started in the 1970s, but it is now included in the Olympic Games. Luckily you don't need to be an Olympic athlete to enjoy it!

There are races for all levels, even beginners. Cross-country racing classes are open to anyone who wants to ride, from elementary school students to grandparents.

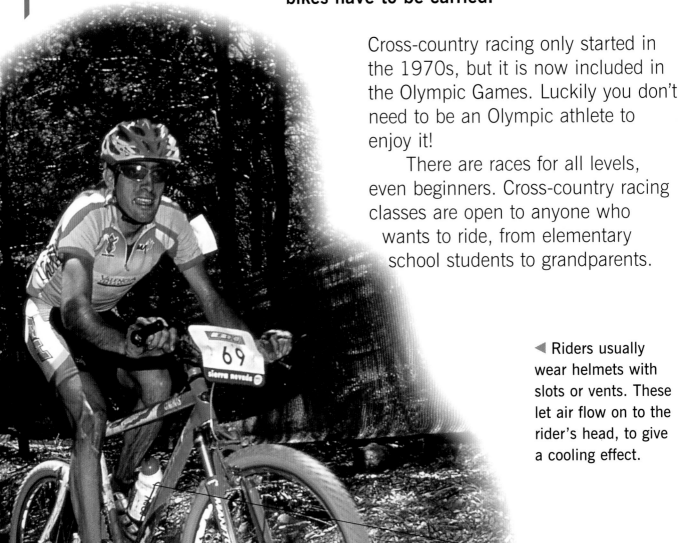

◀ Riders usually wear helmets with slots or vents. These let air flow on to the rider's head, to give a cooling effect.

bottle of water for drinking during the race

◀ Cross-country races include really rough parts, where riders jump off and carry their ATBs.

Tough Tests

Competition riding tests cyclists to their limits. Good training helps a rider to keep going and maybe even win the race.

▲ Some events have very hard sections. In those, riders have to haul their bikes all the way up steep hillsides.

Competition riders train to build up their fitness, strength, and speed.

Fitness is needed if the rider is to keep going throughout a race. Strength is used to zoom up hills, especially the steep ones. And speed is needed to overtake other riders.

▲ Carrying an ATB towards the end of a race tests a rider's strength!

▶ Top riders try to pass slower ones as early as possible in a race. This leaves the course ahead clearer, so they can move toward the front.

Fingerless gloves protect the backs and palms of hands. In winter bare fingertips may get painfully cold.

 ATB fitness tips

Training daily to build up body strength is the best way to get ready for a race. For beginners, such training may be just riding regularly and racing against friends.

Losing body fluid through sweating is bad news, as this reduces muscle power. Some ATB racers suck drinking water from a slim tank, carried on the back like a knapsack.

BMX Freestyle

BMX stands for bicycle motocross. In the 1970s, these small-wheeled machines were the first bikes used for off-road races.

The first BMX bikes were fun machines, and were sold by the million. Today BMX bikes are ridden mostly in serious freestyle events.

Freestyle is the skill of doing stunts, such as jumps and "verting." Here a rider takes off on a steep ramp to do BMX tricks in mid-air.

▲ A rider does a freestyle stunt in mid-air. A good landing is just as important as the stunt.

▶ BMX riders mostly wear soft shoes, so they can feel what the bike is doing. Full-face helmets are usually worn.

rider has pads to protect elbows and knees

BMX bike has smaller wheels than an ATB.

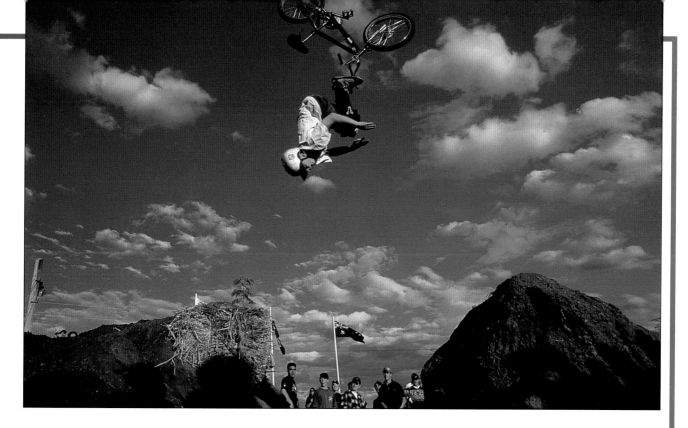

▲ BMX riding is popular worldwide. Here a freestyler competes in the "King of the Dirt" competition in Sydney, Australia.

 BMX words

Here are some popular words from the world of BMX riding:

Aerial Any mid-air freestyle trick.

Endo Balancing on the front wheel.

Peg Metal extension from a wheel axle, used as a foot stand.

Pogo Hopping a bike while balancing it on the front or rear wheel.

Vert Vertical, the best angle off a launch ramp for freestyle tricks.

◀ Advanced riders can carry out aerial stunts like this.

23

New Ideas

New all-terrain bikes and equipment are being developed all the time. New materials allow ATBs to be made lighter, stronger, and often better to ride.

▲ Tiny flashing light units were first made in the 1990s. The extra-bright light makes a bike more visible at night.

Most future ATBs will have both front and rear shock absorbers to make riding easier on rough surfaces.

Frames made of aluminum or carbon fiber will be common. These materials are lighter and stronger than steel. Future ATBs will be better made and easier to ride but will probably cost little more than those of today.

▼ These high-tech tools make repairs an easier job. Wrenches and screwdrivers fold up small enough to tuck in a pocket. The 3 inch (85 mm-) long metal bottle holds enough air to inflate a tire after repair.

*fold-out
screwdriver*

*fold-out
spanner set*

*tire pump
and air bottle*

▶ This design is for a police ATB. The equipment includes a medical kit, a radio, and blue warning lights.

rear shock absorber

front shock absorber

◀ This machine has shock absorbers at front and back, for a smooth ride over rough ground. The frame is a lightweight design, with special high-power brakes.

lightweight pedals

▲ The célérifère was the world's first bicycle.

ATB Facts

Here are some facts and stories from the world of all-terrain bikes.

Early riders

Bicycles go back to the late eighteenth century. In 1791, the French Count de Sivrac built a two-wheeled wooden horse, which he called a célérifère. It was popular for a while, but had no steering, no brakes, and no pedals. In the 1860s a bicycle with pedals was built by the Michaux brothers, in Paris, France. Michaux bikes had no gears, so were quite slow.

Squashy tires

Early bikes had solid wheels that made them very uncomfortable to ride. Many early bicycles were called "boneshakers," because of this. In 1881, a Scot named John Dunlop invented the first pneumatic tire—one made of rubber and filled with air to give a softer ride over bumps. Pneumatic tires made riding so much better that they have been used ever since.

First ATBs

All-terrain bicycles were first developed in the 1970s, when riders went racing down hilly trails in California. There were no ATBs then, so these bikes were handmade. They were called "klunkers" because they seemed heavy and clumsy, compared to the lightweight road bikes of the time.

◀ An ATB tire is made with a deep pattern called a tread. This gives lots of grip on soft ground.

thick rubber tread

◀ Climbing hills is hot work, especially in summer.

Bunny hops

A bunny hop is when a rider jerks a bike's front and back wheels in turn off the ground, to jump over an obstacle. Bunnies were first perfected by BMX riders, and now ATB riders do them, too. The world record is for a hop 44 inches (112.5 cm) off the ground.

Oldest ATB race

In spite of its name, the Road Apple Rally is an off-road ATB race. It was started in 1981 and has been held every year since. The idea behind the first rally was to cycle as far as a horse could cover in one day—about 12 miles (20 km) across rough country—in one hour.

Saving weight

ATB riders have tackled many long-distance trips around the world. On one two-month journey two riders were so ready to save weight that they took no tent or cooking gear. They also cut off the unprinted edges of their trail maps.

Drink up

ATB riding is an energetic sport that involves sweating away body fluid. The body is made mostly of water, so it's very important not to lose too much, otherwise a rider can feel faint or be sick. When riding hard, a rider needs to drink about a quart (1 l) of water an hour.

Friendly to the environment

The bicycle is probably the most efficient vehicle ever invented. A cyclist can ride over 311 miles (500 km), using about the same energy as there is in 1 quart (1 l) of gas. A typical small car can travel about 12 miles (20 km) on the same amount.

▶ This is an ATB with a difference. Instead of wheels, the Austrian machine has skis, and is built for riding on snow, sand, or even grass.

ATB Words

▲ A BMX freestyle trick.

Here are some technical terms used in this book.

aluminum (uh-LOO-mi-nuhm)
A silver metal that is strong, yet light in weight.

ATB
Letters that stand for all-terrain bike. ATBs are often called mountain bikes.

BMX
Letters that stand for bicycle motocross. BMX bikes are smaller and lighter than ATBs. They were first used in the cycling version of moto-cross, an off-road motorcycle sport.

carbon fiber
(KAR-buhn FYE-bur)
The material used in various parts of an ATB. Carbon fiber is usually a plastic with small shreds of carbon added. It is strong and light.

cross-country
(krawss KUHN-tree)
An ATB race that takes place on a winding course, usually with some bits too difficult to ride. Here riders get off and carry their machines.

disc brake (disk brake)
Brake with two pads that grip either side of a metal disc. Cars and motorcycles have used them for many years, but they have been made for ATBs only since the 1990s.

downhill (DOUN-hil)
A type of ATB race that takes place on a winding trail going down a hill. Dual races include both downhill and cross-country sections.

frame (fraym)
Metal "backbone" of an ATB, made of strong tubes that are joined together, usually in a triangular design. On cheap bikes the frame is usually made of steel. More expensive bikes may have frames of aluminium or carbon fiber, that are lighter in weight.

freestyle (FREE-stile)
The sport of making a BMX bike do mid-air tricks.

◀ Most cycle frames have a triangle design because it is very strong.

full-face helmet
(ful-FAYSS HEL-mit)
A type of helmet that covers the head completely, for the best all-round protection in a crash. The wearer looks out through an eye-slit in the front of the helmet.

gear (geer)
System of cogs used on a bike to make pedaling easier. Low gears are used for starting off and for cycling up hills. High gears are for speeding along on the flat and when cycling down hills.

handlebar (HAN-duhl-bar)
Metal cross-tube used to steer a bike. Gear and brake controls are next to the handgrips at each end.

Olympic Games
(oh-LIM-pik gamez)
International games that are held every four years.

pneumatic tire
(new-MAH-tik tire)
Tire that that has an inner rubber tube, filled with air. The inner tube gives slightly to absorb the shock of riding over bumps.

▲ Pneumatic tires and front shock absorbers give this ATB a smooth ride.

shock absorber
(shok ab-ZORB-ur)
A cylinder holding a metal spring, designed to soak up bumps. Many ATBs now have two shock absorbers, one on either side of the front wheel. More expensive ATBs have one for the back wheel, too.

terrain (tuh-RAYN)
Another word for ground.

tread (tred)
Pattern of rubber, molded in a tire. On an ATB, the tread lets the tire sink slightly into the ground for good grip, especially in mud.

wheelie (WEE-lee)
Pulling the front wheel off the ground for a few moments, while keeping the bike balanced on the back wheel.

▲ Many downhill ATBs use disc brakes. (See arrows.)

▲ This bike has a pair
of front shock absorbers.

ATB Science

These experiments show you some of the science in the world of all-terrain bikes.

Bouncing over the bumps

A bike with shock absorbers gives a controlled ride. Inside the metal tube of each shock absorber is a spring that soaks up bumps on the trail.

1 For this mini-experiment all you need is a metal paper clip and a thin tube. A ballpoint pen is just right for the job.

2 Carefully straighten out the paper clip. Hold one end against the ballpoint pen with your thumb. Wrap the clip around the pen.

3 You should end up with a metal spiral. Slide it off the pen, and gently squeeze it between your fingers. Feel the springy bounce!

▲ Oiling moving parts keeps a bike in good condition for riding.

Oil keeps things apart

The moving parts of a bike, such as the wheels, gears, and chain, need to be oiled often.

The oil flows in a thin film between metal parts to reduce friction, or the rubbing action when things touch each other.

1 You need a kitchen cutting board and a square block for this experiment. Here the block is made from toy building bricks.

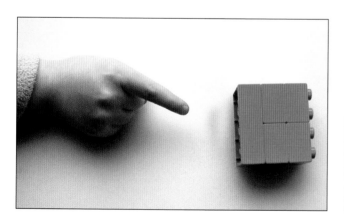

2 Lay the block on the board and flick it with your finger. The block moves but soon stops. Now pour a little oil on the board.

3 You will find that a flick now sends the block much farther. The oil reduces friction by keeping the block and board slightly apart.

Index

aluminum 6, 24, 28
ATB science 30, 31

BMX 22, 23, 27, 28
"boneshakers" 26
brakes 6, 7, 12, 16, 25, 26, 29
bunny hop 27

camera 10, 11
carbon fiber 24, 28
célérifère 26
chain 7, 31
cruiser bike 6

drinking 10, 18, 21, 27

frame 6, 28

gears 7, 26, 29, 31
glasses 12, 18
gloves 21

handlebars 6, 29
helmets 12, 17, 18, 22, 29

"klunkers" 26

lights 11, 24

Olympic Games 18, 19, 29

pedals 6, 7, 25, 26
people
    Dunlop, John 26
    Michaux brothers 26
    Sivrac, Count de 26
places
    Andes, South America 14
    California 26
    Paris, France 26
    Peru, South America 14
    Rocky Mountains 11
    Sahara desert, Africa 15
    San Francisco 4
    Switzerland 17
    Sydney, Australia 23

police ATB 25
pump 8, 24
puncture repair kit 8

racing
    competition 20, 21
    cross-country 5, 18, 19, 28
    downhill 4, 5, 16, 17, 28
    "King of the Dirt" 23
    Road Apple Rally 27

shock absorbers 6, 24, 25, 29, 30
steel 6, 24, 28
steering 26

tires 6, 7, 8, 17, 26, 29
tools 8, 24
trail 10, 11, 12, 15, 19, 28
tread 6, 26, 29

wheels 6, 7, 22, 26
wheelie 2, 29